SCHOLASTIC

MAIN IDEAS & SUMMARIZING

by Linda Ward Beech

NEW YORK • TORONTO • LONDON • AUCKLAND • SYDNEY
MEXICO CITY • NEW DELHI • HONG KONG • BUENOS AIRES

Teaching *Resources*

Cover design by Maria Lilja
Interior design by Sydney Wright
Interior illustrations by Mike Gordon

ISBN-13 978-0-439-55412-1
ISBN-10 0-439-55412-8

16 15   40   14 13 12

Contents

Introduction

Reading comprehension involves numerous thinking skills. Identifying main ideas and the details that support them is one such skill. A reader who is adept at identifying main ideas makes better sense of a text and increases his or her comprehension of what is being communicated. Identifying main ideas is one step in reading nonfiction, but it is important that students go further. They should also be able to use main ideas to summarize information. By summarizing as they read, students will be better able to recall important points. Exercises 1–18 will help students learn to recognize main ideas and the details that develop them. Exercises 19–35 focus on practice in summarizing. Use pages 8 and 9 after you introduce the skills to give students help in understanding them.

Using This Book

Pages 8–9

After introducing main ideas and summarizing to students (see pages 6 and 7), duplicate and pass out pages 8 and 9. Use page 8 to help students review what they have learned about finding main ideas and supporting details. By explaining their thinking, students are using metacognition to analyze how they recognized main ideas. Page 9 helps students review what they have learned about summarizing.

Pages 10–27

These pages provide practice in identifying **main ideas** and supporting details. The first question for each passage asks students to identify the main idea, and the second question requires students to focus on supporting details. Tell students that some passages have explicit main ideas, which are stated in a sentence, while other passages have implicit main ideas, which require students to put the details together to determine the main idea. Students should fill in the bubble in front of the correct answer for each question.

Pages 28–44

These pages provide practice in **summarizing**. The first three questions help students identify the key information in the paragraph. The fourth question asks students to select the title that best summarizes the passage. Finally, students are asked to use their answers to summarize the information given.

Pages 45–46

Use these pages to assess students' progress after they have completed the practice pages.

Page 47

You may wish to keep a record of students' progress as they complete the practice pages. Sample comments that will help you guide students to improving their skills might include:

- reads carelessly
- misunderstands text
- doesn't recognize main ideas
- has trouble differentiating main ideas from supporting details
- is weak in summarizing material

Teacher Tip

For students who need extra help, you might suggest that they keep pages 8 and 9 with them to refer to when they complete the exercises.

Teacher Tip

Students can learn a lot if you review the finished exercises with them on a regular basis. Encourage students to explain their thinking for each correct answer. Ask them to point out the words that helped them identify main ideas.

Teaching About Main Ideas (and Supporting Details)

1. Introduce the concept: Write these words on the chalkboard.

ocean   lagoon   bay   pond   creek

2. Model thinking: After students have correctly identified bodies of water as what the words are about, continue the lesson by thinking aloud.

Each of the words is a geographic term.

Each word names a different body of water.

3. Define the skill: Remind students that when they read a paragraph, the sentences in it are related to one another. The sentences are all about a main idea. This is the key point in the paragraph. Explain that often the main idea is stated in the first sentence of a paragraph, but the main idea can also be given in the middle or at the end of a paragraph.

Tell students that the other sentences in a paragraph tell more about the main idea. These sentences give supporting details. A supporting detail might be an example. It might also be a fact about the main idea or a description of it. Explain that supporting details fill in information about the main idea and make the paragraph more interesting to read. Help students understand that the main idea is bigger or broader than the supporting details.

Point out that sometimes the main idea is *not* stated in a single sentence. Instead, all the details suggest the main idea; in other words, the main idea is implied, as in the example above. Then the reader must figure it out by asking questions such as "What is happening?" "What is this about?"

Use graphics to help students who are visual learners understand the concept.

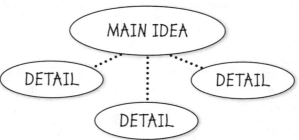

Teaching About Summarizing

1. Introduce the concept: Draw five pictures on the board that convey the power of wind. (You may also create an overhead transparency using the illustrations below.)

Ask students to make up a sentence that tells about all the pictures.

2. Model thinking: After students have volunteered their sentences, help them review the process they used by thinking aloud.

All the pictures show what happens when the wind blows.

The power of the wind is the main idea suggested in each picture.

I might summarize this group of pictures by saying, *The wind is strong and can make things move.*

3. Define the skill: Explain that summarizing is a way to remember what you read (or see or hear). When you summarize, you look for the main ideas. Then you try to state or restate them in your own words. Tell students that adding details to a summary can be helpful. For example, you might say, *The wind is strong and can make things such as a kite move.*

Tell students that outlines and graphic organizers are often good ways to summarize information. For example:

I. The power of the wind
  A. Bends trees
  B. Carries away hats
  C. Turns umbrellas inside out
  D. Helps kites fly
  E. Makes boats move

What Is a Main Idea?

When you read a nonfiction passage, it usually gives you a lot of information. How does a reader remember all this information? How does a reader make sense of it?

A good reader sorts out the information. For example, a reader might think:

What is the "big picture" in this passage? What is the main point of it?

What other information is given? How does it help me understand the main point?

When you answer the first two questions, you identify the main idea. The main idea is what the paragraph is about. When you answer the second two questions, you identify the supporting details. These details tell more about the main idea by describing or explaining *what, where, why, how much, when, who,* or *how many.*

Read the passage. Complete the statements.

Can snakes crawl in reverse? Well, no, but they can move in other ways. For example, they can sidewind, which involves throwing the front of their body to one side and then zigzagging the rest along the ground. Some snakes such as pythons can climb trees, and some vipers can actually leap. Many snakes can swim, too.

1 This passage is mainly about _____

_____

2 One detail about the main idea is _____

_____

3 Another detail about the main idea is _____

_____

4 The details help me understand the main idea because they _____

_____

Scholastic Teaching Resources *Main Ideas & Summarizing*

What Is Summarizing?

When you read nonfiction, you want to remember what you read. However, it isn't necessary to recall every word. Instead, you can use the main ideas to help you summarize a passage.

A good reader first finds the main ideas. Keep in mind that the main points are not always stated; sometimes they are implied or suggested. After finding the main ideas, a reader might think:

How can I restate the main idea in my own words?

The next thing a reader does is to identify supporting evidence for the main idea. This evidence can be details, examples, explanations, descriptions, or statistics that expand the main idea. Often, it is helpful to use an outline or a graphic organizer to summarize information.

Read this passage. Complete the statements.

Where is the Grand Canyon? Most people think it is in Arizona. However, many other states have their own grand canyons, too. The Waimea Canyon is known as the Grand Canyon of Hawaii. People in North Dakota think of the Painted Canyon in that state as their grand canyon. And Californians use the nickname for a canyon on the floor of the Pacific Ocean. This underwater grand canyon is officially called the Monterey Bay Canyon.

1 This paragraph is mainly about _____

_____

_____

2 A good title for this paragraph would be _____

_____

3 A detail I might include in a summary would be _____

_____

Main Ideas

Read each paragraph. Choose the best answers.

You probably know that guide dogs are used to lead blind people. Did you know that a few blind people have guide horses? These are miniature horses trained much as guide dogs are. The small horses respond to more than 25 commands. They can see well in the dark. They are also trained to tap with a hoof on the door if they need to go out. One man has even taken his guide horse on an airplane!

1 The main idea of this paragraph is

(A) How guide dogs are trained

(B) A guide horse on an airplane

(C) The use of small horses as guides

(D) Why blind people like animals

2 A supporting detail is

(A) Guide dogs lead blind people.

(B) The horses respond to 25 commands.

(C) Miniature means small.

(D) Airlines welcome guide horses.

Dictionary writers are always busy. That's because the English language keeps changing. People stop using some words, and new words keep popping up. Where do new words come from? Many recent words are from technology. For example, *snailmail* came into use after people started using the much faster e-mail. Other new words come from books, television, movies, and fads. Do you know what a *wannabe* is? If not, you can look it up in a recently published dictionary.

3 The main idea of this paragraph is

(A) Dictionaries show changes in English.

(B) How television affects English

(C) Why dictionary writers are so tired

(D) How to find new words in a dictionary

4 A supporting detail is

(A) Snails help to deliver the mail.

(B) Many words come from technology.

(C) Old dictionaries are not useful.

(D) The English language never changes.

Main Ideas

Read each paragraph. Choose the best answers.

Ashrita Furman likes to break records. In fact, over the years Furman has set or broken more than 79 records listed in the *Guinness Book of World Records*. Two of his feats include race-walking the fastest mile while twirling a hula hoop and walking 81 miles with a milk bottle on top of his head. He has also held records for balancing 75 glasses on his chin and for going up and down Mt. Fuji in Japan on a pogo stick. Why? Mr. Furman feels these activities bring him inner peace.

1 The main idea of this paragraph is
- (A) The *Guinness Book of World Records*
- (B) How to walk with a bottle on your head
- (C) Climbing Japan's Mt. Fuji
- (D) Ashrita Furman likes to break records.

2 A supporting detail is
- (A) Reading about world record holders
- (B) Selling the most hit records
- (C) Record for balancing glasses on chin
- (D) The prizes won by Ashrita Furman

In 2003 scientists sighted a new object in our solar system. This object, which scientists are calling Sedna, is far beyond Pluto and takes 10,500 years to orbit the sun. Sedna is very cold—minus 400 degrees Fahrenheit—and has a reddish color. It also appears to be shiny. Scientists believe this astronomical body is made up of ancient rock and ice. Is Sedna a planet? Not exactly. For now, scientists are calling it a planetoid.

3 The main idea of this paragraph is
- (A) A planet of primitive rock and ice
- (B) Scientists find Sedna in our solar system.
- (C) Orbiting bodies in our solar system
- (D) Sedna is almost as red as Mars.

4 A supporting detail is
- (A) Our solar system has a new object.
- (B) Sedna takes 10,500 years to orbit the sun.
- (C) The real Sedna was an Inuit goddess.
- (D) The planetoid is close to Pluto.

Main Ideas

Read each paragraph. Choose the best answers.

Where do you build the world's largest jet airliner? First, you have to put up the world's largest building. That's just what happened in Everett, Washington. An airplane factory there covers more than 98 acres under one roof. More than 75 NFL football fields could fit inside! More than 15 railcars a day deliver parts to the factory. Workers use overhead cranes and forklifts to assemble the large pieces. Buyers from all over the world purchase the finished airplanes.

1 The main idea of this paragraph is

   (A) Looking for the largest jet airliner   (C) Railcars deliver parts to the factory.

   (B) The largest building is a jet factory.   (D) How to build airplanes indoors

2 A supporting detail is

   (A) Choosing a place to build a factory   (C) Visitors can tour the huge factory.

   (B) Teams play football in the building.   (D) The factory covers about 98 acres.

People in ancient Egypt celebrated many different kinds of festivals. Some of these honored nature. For example, there were festivals when the Nile River flooded, making the riverbanks fertile for farming. Other festivals were celebrated at the beginning of spring and at harvest time. At the celebrations families enjoyed foods such as watermelon, grapes, and figs that were sold at stalls. People also listened to musicians and watched entertainers such as acrobats.

3 The main idea of this paragraph is

   (A) Why the Nile was important to Egypt   (C) Ancient Egypt had many festivals.

   (B) Watermelon was sold at food stalls.   (D) The festivals honored nature.

4 A supporting detail is

   (A) Egyptians honored their ancestors.   (C) The Feast of Opet lasted a month.

   (B) All Egypt's festivals honored nature.   (D) People were entertained at the festivals.

Main Ideas

Read each paragraph. Choose the best answers.

A jingle dress is for special occasions among the Ojibwa people. Often, Ojibwa women and girls wear a jingle dress at powwows. These are social gatherings where people do traditional dances and have fun. A jingle dress has small metal cones hanging from it like a fringe. The dress makes a jingling sound when a girl dances. According to a story, a jingle dress helped to cure a young girl. That is why the Ojibwa believe that the jingle dress is a healing garment.

1 The main idea of this paragraph is

(A) The dress makes a jingling sound.

(B) People get cured from jingle dresses.

(C) A jingle dress is for special Ojibwa events.

(D) A powwow is a social gathering.

2 A supporting detail is

(A) The dress has a fringe of metal cones.

(B) The Ojibwa are from the Great Lakes.

(C) People camp out at powwows.

(D) The Ojibwa wear jingle dresses.

The hippopotamus spends a lot of time in water. In fact, the name of this large African animal means "river horse." During a hot day, a hippo will spend its hours in rivers and lakes. Only its eyes, ears, and nostrils can be seen above the water. This helps to keep the hairless animal from getting sunburned. Although it eats water plants, the hippo goes ashore at night to find larger plants. If it is the dry season and the water is low, hippos roll in mud to cover their large bodies. This way their skin doesn't dry out.

3 The main idea of this paragraph is

(A) A hippopotamus is a water horse.

(B) This animal eats water and land plants.

(C) Hippos live only in Africa.

(D) A hippo spends a lot of time in water.

4 A supporting detail is

(A) Sometimes hippos overturn boats.

(B) Sunburn is a problem for many animals.

(C) Water plants are good for hippos.

(D) Water protects a hippo's skin from the sun.

Main Ideas

Read each paragraph. Choose the best answers.

Do you eat breakfast every day? Researchers have found that people who eat a balanced breakfast are likely to be healthier than those who don't. One reason is that most people eat whole grains at breakfast, and these promote good health. Breakfast eaters also tend to have fewer weight problems than those who skip the meal. People who don't eat breakfast usually eat too much later in the day. Often, these foods are not healthy and cause weight gain and other problems. So, be sure to eat breakfast. It is the most important meal of the day.

1 The main idea of this paragraph is

  Ⓐ Breakfast is the most important meal.   Ⓒ Breakfast is a delicious meal.

  Ⓑ Skipping breakfast makes you hungry.   Ⓓ Breakfast eaters have fewer weight problems.

2 A supporting detail is

  Ⓐ People eat too much at lunch.   Ⓒ Only healthy people eat breakfast.

  Ⓑ No one has time to eat breakfast.   Ⓓ Whole grains at breakfast promote health.

Once, shoes were made entirely by hand. The hardest step was connecting the upper part of a shoe to the innersole. A worker had to stretch the leather over a wooden form called a *last*. Jan Matzeliger changed all that in the 1880s. He invented a lasting machine to do this difficult work. Matzeliger's machine meant that many more shoes could be made in a day than before and for less money. The price of shoes came down, and more people could afford them.

3 The main idea of this paragraph is

  Ⓐ Once shoes were made by hand.   Ⓒ Matzeliger changed how shoes are made.

  Ⓑ Jan Matzeliger was an inventor.   Ⓓ More people could now afford shoes.

4 A supporting detail is

  Ⓐ What Matzeliger's machine looked like   Ⓒ Some people went barefoot.

  Ⓑ Lasting is a difficult step in shoemaking.   Ⓓ The 1880s were a time of change.

Scholastic Teaching Resources   *Main Ideas & Summarizing*

Main Ideas

Read each paragraph. Choose the best answers.

Have you ever carried a stone around in your pocket? According to a tradition of the Seneca, a favorite stone can tell something about you. If your stone is smooth, it means you are gentle. A rough stone means that you follow creative ideas. Gray stones suggest that you are friendly, while brown ones mean you love nature. The shape of your stone has meaning too. A round stone says you are flexible. Is your stone oval? You are seeking a better life.

1 The main idea of this paragraph is

Ⓐ It's good to carry stones in your pocket.   Ⓒ Rough stones mean creativity.

Ⓑ Stones are precious possessions.   Ⓓ Stones have meaning to the Seneca.

2 A supporting detail is

Ⓐ Everyone should carry a stone.   Ⓒ Stones are found in many colors.

Ⓑ Brown stones mean you love nature.   Ⓓ A stone's shape is not important.

Lions live together in social groups called prides. Most of the lions in a pride are females and their cubs. The lionesses share the work of hunting and raising the cubs. By hunting in a pack, lions can take down animals far larger than themselves. Much of the food killed by a pride is taken by the males. In return, they provide protection from other males. A pride has a well-defined territory, which is marked by the males. When lions in a pride meet, they greet one another by head rubbing, licking, and grooming.

3 The main idea of this paragraph is

Ⓐ Males eat most of a pride's food.   Ⓒ Lions hunt together in a pack.

Ⓑ Lions live in groups called prides.   Ⓓ Lionesses share the work of a pride.

4 A supporting detail is

Ⓐ The males mark a pride's territory.   Ⓒ Cubs are helpless when they're born.

Ⓑ The pride is a lion's family group.   Ⓓ Lions are solitary hunters.

Main Ideas

Read each paragraph. Choose the best answers.

A roller brigade glides down a boulevard in Paris. This group of inline skaters is part of the city's police force. Their job is to keep bus lanes free of passenger cars on busy streets. They also pull over drivers who are chatting on mobile phones. The best part of their work is posing for pictures with tourists. The *rolleurs* wear helmets and knee pads as part of their uniform. Even so, it can be tricky to navigate some streets in Paris, especially those paved with cobblestones.

1 The main idea of this paragraph is

Ⓐ Paris has a lot of automobile traffic.

Ⓒ Some police in Paris work on skates.

Ⓑ A *rolleur* wears a helmet and pads.

Ⓓ Inline skates are not just for fun.

2 A supporting detail is

Ⓐ Police departments try new things.

Ⓒ Inline police keep bus lanes free.

Ⓑ Tourists visit Paris to see the police.

Ⓓ Cobblestones make driving difficult.

Eyeglasses have an interesting history. Early Greek scientists observed that when filled with water, a glass ball magnified objects held beneath it. The Romans used certain rocks to magnify things and aid their vision. The emperor Nero wore an emerald ring for this purpose. By the twelfth century, the Chinese had invented eyeglasses made with rock crystal lenses. Later, in Europe, eyeglasses became a big fad. If a king wore them, so did everyone else.

3 The main idea of this paragraph is

Ⓐ The early history of eyeglasses

Ⓒ Wearing eyeglasses as fashion

Ⓑ The secret of Nero's emerald ring

Ⓓ Vision aids have a rocky start.

4 A supporting detail is

Ⓐ The story of magnification

Ⓒ An interesting study of rocks

Ⓑ From rocks to fashion statements

Ⓓ The Chinese invented eyeglasses.

Main Ideas

Read each paragraph. Choose the best answers.

At one time children in Nicaragua with hearing impairments were kept hidden. They were not taught any form of communication. Finally, in 1979, the government of this Latin American country set up two schools for these children. At first, the children could not understand their teachers. But they soon began communicating among themselves with their hands. They developed more and more signs or signals. New students learned them too. Today Nicaraguan Sign Language is a recognized language.

1 The main idea of this paragraph is

Ⓐ Nicaragua is in Latin America.

Ⓒ Children deserve to go to school.

Ⓑ Children developed a sign language.

Ⓓ How teachers and students communicate

2 A supporting detail is

Ⓐ Children communicated with hands.

Ⓒ The students learned to speak.

Ⓑ The students hid from their teachers.

Ⓓ Many people have hearing problems.

What is the history of Father's Day? This holiday was first suggested by Sonora Smart Dodd in the early 1900s. She told her idea to people in her hometown of Spokane, Washington, and they began celebrating it. However, the holiday did not spread, and by the 1920s it had died out. Then in 1938 some men's clothing stores began promoting Father's Day as a way to raise sales. They used the slogan "Give Dad Something to Wear." In 1972, Father's Day finally became a national holiday.

3 The main idea of this paragraph is

Ⓐ Giving clothes on Father's Day

Ⓒ The holiday that died out

Ⓑ A national holiday in 1972

Ⓓ A history of Father's Day

4 A supporting detail is

Ⓐ A family holiday in June

Ⓒ Sonora Smart Dodd suggests an idea.

Ⓑ Why fathers wear fashionable clothes

Ⓓ Send greeting cards on Father's Day.

Main Ideas

Read each paragraph. Choose the best answers.

In the days of ancient Rome, taking a bath was a social event. Romans of all classes bathed in large public bathhouses. These buildings were decorated with mosaic floors, marble walls, and painted walls. There were hot baths, warm baths, cold baths, and hot-dry baths for sweating. People met their friends, heard the news, and got clean all at the same time. Sometimes bathers even held business meetings!

1 The main idea of this paragraph is

(A) Business meetings in ancient Rome

(B) Public bathhouses in ancient Rome

(C) Decorations in Roman bathhouses

(D) How Romans got clean long ago

2 A supporting detail is

(A) Bathers used sponges and oils.

(B) Roman plumbing was efficient.

(C) Bathhouses had mosaic floors.

(D) Roman baths were only for the rich.

Reefs and atolls are formed from masses of coral that surround volcanic islands. Over many years, a volcanic island gradually sinks but the masses of coral grow upward and form a barrier between the island and the sea. The water between the island and the reef is called a lagoon. When the island completely sinks from view, the reef continues to grow and often forms a circle around the lagoon. This is called an atoll. The Pacific Ocean has many atolls.

3 The main idea of this paragraph is

(A) How lagoons are formed

(B) What barrier reefs are made of

(C) What happens to volcanic islands

(D) How reefs and atolls are formed

4 A supporting detail is

(A) The Pacific Ocean has many atolls.

(B) A lagoon has warm water.

(C) Reefs cause islands to sink.

(D) Reefs and atolls grow quickly.

Scholastic Teaching Resources   *Main Ideas & Summarizing*

Main Ideas

Read each paragraph. Choose the best answers.

People have used oil since early times. Ancient cultures learned that oil was sticky and useful for binding things together. They also noted that oil kept water out. For example, the Sumerians used the oil in asphalt to keep mosaics on walls and in floors. The people of Mesopotamia used the oil in bitumen to seal the joints in wooden boats. Other groups found that oil burned well to create light. Throughout the ages, hundreds of other uses for oil were discovered.

1 The main idea of this paragraph is

(A) The Sumerians used oil as glue.

(B) When burned, oil creates light.

(C) Oil has sticky qualities.

(D) People have used oil through the ages.

2 A supporting detail is

(A) The Chinese found oil underground.

(B) Mesopotamians used oil as a sealer.

(C) People learned that oil is useful.

(D) Oil is a precious resource.

What is a gaggle? You probably know that it is a group of geese. *Gaggle* is a collective noun because it names a group. Many collective nouns name groups of animals. For example, a string is a group of ponies, and a troop is a group of kangaroos. What is a knot? If you're talking about toads, then a knot is a group of them. Have you ever found foxes together? Then you saw a skulk. And if a group of elk crosses in front of you, you're looking at a gang.

3 The main idea of this paragraph is

(A) Meanings of collective nouns

(B) A knot is a group of toads.

(C) Names for different animals

(D) How to use collective nouns

4 A supporting detail is

(A) Ants live in a colony.

(B) A gang is a group of elk.

(C) Words with two meanings

(D) Singular and plural nouns

Main Ideas

Read each paragraph. Choose the best answers.

William Steig (1907–2003) was known for his cartoons and his children's books. For more than six decades, his cartoons amused readers of *The New Yorker* magazine. He was also responsible for the drawings on many of the publication's covers. Steig started writing and illustrating books for children in the 1970s. Some of his most famous titles include *Sylvester and the Magic Pebble, CDC?, Dr. DeSoto,* and *Amos and Boris.* One of his book characters—Shrek—has starred in popular movies of the same name.

1 The main idea of this paragraph is
- Ⓐ The work of William Steig
- Ⓑ The cartoons of William Steig
- Ⓒ The life of William Steig
- Ⓓ The books of William Steig

2 A supporting detail is
- Ⓐ Steig lived a long life.
- Ⓑ Steig wrote *New Yorker* articles.
- Ⓒ Steig wrote the book *Dr. DeSoto.*
- Ⓓ Steig enjoyed making movies.

Thanks to the St. Lawrence Seaway, ships can carry cargo from Duluth, Minnesota, to the Atlantic Ocean. The trip covers 2,700 nautical miles. To create the Seaway, the St. Lawrence River had to be excavated. A 27-foot-deep channel between the city of Montreal and Lake Ontario was dug. Many locks were built so that ships could be raised or lowered as the height of the water changed on the route. Canals, roads, and bridges were built as well. The Seaway officially opened in 1959.

3 The main idea of this paragraph is
- Ⓐ Building the St. Lawrence Seaway
- Ⓑ A 2,700-mile nautical journey
- Ⓒ Building locks for ships
- Ⓓ Expanding the St. Lawrence River

4 A supporting detail is
- Ⓐ Connecting the U.S. and Canada
- Ⓑ The locks are made of concrete.
- Ⓒ The Seaway opened in 1959.
- Ⓓ Ships carry tons of freight.

Scholastic Teaching Resources   *Main Ideas & Summarizing*

Main Ideas

Read each paragraph. Choose the best answers.

Happy New Year! People say this all over the world; however, not everyone celebrates this day in the same way. In Iceland, New Year's Eve is a time to clean up trash and perform elf dances. Families in Ecuador dance around scarecrows and read lists of people's faults. Later, when they set the scarecrow on fire, both it and the faults go up in flames. In Belgium, children write down good deeds they hope to perform. Chinese and Japanese get off to a good start by paying all their debts. How do you celebrate?

1 The main idea of this paragraph is

(A) Performing good deeds in Belgium

(B) New Year's traditions around the world

(C) How Americans celebrate the New Year

(D) A time to pay off debts

2 A supporting detail is

(A) How to celebrate the New Year

(B) January 1 is a national holiday.

(C) Learning to do elf dances

(D) Icelanders clean up trash.

Some expressions about feelings are very colorful! If you're sad, you might be "feeling blue." Have you ever been so excited that you "talked a blue streak"? Perhaps you were "tickled pink." If you've ever been jealous, you might have been "green with envy." Suppose you are scared. Then you might turn "white as a sheet." Anger might make you "see red." Embarrassed about something? Will you turn "red as a beet"?

3 The main idea of this paragraph is

(A) Using blue to describe feelings

(B) "Seeing red" means being angry.

(C) Idioms about unhappy feelings

(D) Color phrases help express feelings.

4 A supporting detail is

(A) Understanding English sayings

(B) A rainbow of expressions

(C) "Green with envy" expresses jealousy.

(D) Yellow often means cowardice.

Main Ideas

Read each paragraph. Choose the best answers.

Not everyone in the world uses the same calendar. If you are a Hindu, you follow the Hindu calendar. It has 360 days divided into 12 months of 30 days each. The months are counted from full moon to full moon. A leap month is added every five years to keep the calendar in line with the seasons. Each month has two parts; Krsna is the first part, when the moon is getting smaller, and Sukla is the second part, when the moon is getting fuller. Some names of months are Chaitra, Asadha, and Pausa.

1 The main idea of this paragraph is

Ⓐ Calendars around the world

Ⓑ The two parts of a Hindu month

Ⓒ Understanding the Hindu calendar

Ⓓ A year of 12 months

2 A supporting detail is

Ⓐ Chaitra is one Hindu month.

Ⓑ Special Hindu holidays

Ⓒ Naming the Hindu months

Ⓓ Kinds of Hindu calendars

If you are a movie fan, you probably watch the Oscars on television. These awards for excellence in the film industry were first given in 1929. At that time there was no TV. Instead, 250 people attended a banquet in Hollywood sponsored by the Academy of Motion Picture Arts and Sciences. The winning film that year was *Wings*, a war story. As for the name Oscar, a secretary at the academy said the statue looked like her Uncle Oscar.

3 The main idea of this paragraph is

Ⓐ How the Oscars were named

Ⓑ What movie fans do

Ⓒ The first Oscar awards

Ⓓ *Wings* won the first film award.

4 A supporting detail is

Ⓐ How to win an Oscar award

Ⓑ The first Oscars were in 1929.

Ⓒ Watching the Oscars on television

Ⓓ Why the Oscars are popular

Main Ideas

Read each paragraph. Choose the best answers.

You turn a year older, and friends sing a certain song to you. The story of "Happy Birthday" goes back to the 1890s. In 1893 a teacher named Patty Smith Hill and her sister Mildred published a book called *Song Stories for Kindergarten*. The first song in the book was a four-line verse called "Good Morning to All." Patty soon wrote new words to this ditty, and it became the popular "Happy Birthday" song still sung today. People sing it in many languages around the world.

1 The main idea of this paragraph is

Ⓐ Celebrating birthdays

Ⓑ Kindergarten songs

Ⓒ The story of "Happy Birthday"

Ⓓ A worldwide birthday song

2 A supporting detail is

Ⓐ Mildred Hill was a church organist.

Ⓑ Patty Hill wrote the words.

Ⓒ Kindergartners like to sing.

Ⓓ People in Nepal sing the song.

When the first rail lines were put in place across the United States in 1869, officials had a problem. Each town along the way set its clock by the noonday sun. So the time was never the same from place to place. It was hard to have a reliable railroad schedule with this system. So in 1883, railroad owners, scientists, and businessmen came up with four time zones across the country. This new system was called Standard Railway Time. Today, these are the time zones in use across the United States.

3 The main idea of this paragraph is

Ⓐ The first transcontinental railroad

Ⓑ Trains that were never on time

Ⓒ Different times in different places

Ⓓ How railroads resulted in time zones

4 A supporting detail is

Ⓐ Standard Railway Time was set up.

Ⓑ Sometimes the sun didn't shine.

Ⓒ There were 80 time zones in 1869.

Ⓓ Towns built railroad stations.

Main Ideas

Read each paragraph. Choose the best answers.

In the 1860s an American named Henry Bergh was in Russia working for the U.S. government. He was horrified when he saw local peasants beating their horses in the streets. Soon after that, Bergh founded an organization in the United States to help animals. It was called the American Society for the Prevention of Cruelty to Animals (ASPCA). As the first president, Bergh worked hard to keep people from abusing animals. He even started an ambulance service for horses. It began two years before there was one for people.

1 The main idea of this paragraph is

   (A) What Bergh saw in Russia

   (B) The life story of Henry Bergh

   (C) The first horse ambulance

   (D) How the ASPCA was started

2 A supporting detail is

   (A) Bergh was the first president.

   (B) Horses pulled carriages and wagons.

   (C) Bergh was a wealthy man.

   (D) The ASPCA still exists.

The Smithsonian Institution opened in Washington, D.C., in 1855. It is the world's largest museum and covers 19 acres. It was founded because of the generosity of an Englishman named James Smithson. When Smithson died in 1829, he left his money to a nephew. If the nephew had no heirs, the money was to go to the U.S. government to start a museum. The nephew died in 1835, leaving no children. And sure enough, 105 bags of gold arrived in the United States for the museum. Curiously, Smithson never visited this country.

3 The main idea of this paragraph is

   (A) What the Smithsonian is like

   (B) The origin of the Smithsonian

   (C) Who was James Smithson?

   (D) The world's largest museum

4 A supporting detail is

   (A) Place of interest in the United States

   (B) The Smithsonian includes a zoo.

   (C) Bags of gold arrived for the museum.

   (D) Smithson loved Washington, D.C.

Scholastic Teaching Resources   *Main Ideas & Summarizing*

Main Ideas

Read each paragraph. Choose the best answers.

Many words have interesting stories about their origins. For example, the Cesar Ritz was a fancy hotel in Switzerland. The word *ritzy* came to mean "very fancy." In Greek mythology, Atlas was a giant who had to hold the world on his shoulders. Today, an atlas is a book of maps. A vandal is someone who destroys things on purpose. This word comes from the Vandals who were known for attacking and robbing their neighbors in ancient Europe.

1 The main idea of this paragraph is

   (A) How the word *atlas* came into use

   (B) Interesting word histories

   (C) Words from Greek mythology

   (D) Words that come from places

2 A supporting detail is

   (A) How people use words

   (B) The story of the English language

   (C) *Ritzy* comes from a hotel name.

   (D) Where the word *cereal* originated

A census is a counting of a nation's population. The first census in the United States took place in 1790. Riders on horseback fanned out over the country for 18 months to count the inhabitants. They came up with almost four million people. Only 12 cities had more than 5,000 residents. New York, Philadelphia, Boston, and Charleston had more than 16,000 each. The states with the highest populations were Virginia and Pennsylvania.

3 The main idea of this paragraph is

   (A) Results of the first U.S. census

   (B) How the United States has grown

   (C) Why the census was taken

   (D) The biggest cities in 1790

4 A supporting detail is

   (A) Many people weren't counted.

   (B) Maryland had the most people.

   (C) Most people lived in rural areas.

   (D) The census took a year and a half.

Main Ideas

Read each paragraph. Choose the best answers.

Many towns in the United States have landforms as part of their names. For example, there's Farmington Hills in Michigan and White Plains in New York. California has a town named La Mesa, while Kentucky offers Valley Station. There's also Council Bluffs in Iowa, Eden Prairie in Minnesota, and Pine Ridge in Mississippi. And don't overlook Swampscott. That's in Massachusetts.

1 The main idea of this paragraph is
- (A) Places with landform names
- (B) Unusual names for U.S. towns
- (C) Valley Station is in Kentucky.
- (D) A variety of landforms

2 A supporting detail is
- (A) Many states have mountains.
- (B) Places often reflect landforms.
- (C) A mesa is a flat-topped plateau.
- (D) Pine Ridge is in Mississippi.

Most people take their mail delivery for granted, but this wasn't always the case. Before the Civil War (1861–1865), people had to pick up their mail at the post office. As the war casualties mounted, the lines grew longer and longer. A clerk named Joseph Briggs in Cleveland, Ohio, began delivering mail to the homes of soldiers. Soon, he was campaigning for free home delivery for everyone. At first the idea was thought to be too expensive. But free door-to-door delivery began in Cleveland and 41 other cities in 1863.

3 The main idea of this paragraph is
- (A) War casualties grew in the Civil War.
- (B) Briggs delivered mail in Cleveland.
- (C) How home mail delivery got started
- (D) People take mail delivery for granted.

4 A supporting detail is
- (A) Mail delivery began in Cleveland.
- (B) Soldiers deserved free mail delivery.
- (C) Most people hate to wait in line.
- (D) Few people got letters in the 1860s.

Main Ideas

Read each paragraph. Choose the best answers.

When the first English settlers arrived in America, they were amazed at the foods they found. The Indians had developed techniques for growing corn, squash, watermelons, and other crops. The settlers also found blueberries, cranberries, wild rice, and pumpkin. They learned to eat lobster and crab as well as cod and striped bass. Still other foods included nuts such as cashews, black walnuts, hickory nuts, and pecans. Wild turkeys were also a first for the settlers.

1 The main idea of this paragraph is

(A) Local foods found by English settlers

(B) How Indians caught seafood

(C) A variety of new nuts to eat

(D) Berries were plentiful.

2 A supporting detail is

(A) A new menu for the settlers

(B) The settlers ate their first turkey.

(C) Kidney and lima beans were good.

(D) Native foods were delicious.

Many U.S. presidents have had nicknames. Calvin Coolidge was known as Silent Cal because he rarely spoke. The Little Magician was Martin Van Buren, who wore a tall silk hat. Grover Cleveland earned the nickname Veto President because he vetoed more bills than all previous presidents combined. Andrew Jackson's nickname was Old Hickory, while Theodore Roosevelt's was Rough Rider. The Great Emancipator was Abraham Lincoln, who wrote a proclamation that emancipated, or freed, slaves.

3 The main idea of this paragraph is

(A) Grover Cleveland vetoed many bills.

(B) Not all nicknames are flattering.

(C) Many presidents have had nicknames.

(D) Everyone should have a nickname.

4 A supporting detail is

(A) Nicknames are given fondly.

(B) Calvin Coolidge was talkative.

(C) Lincoln was the greatest president.

(D) Andrew Jackson was Old Hickory.

Summarizing

Read the paragraph. Answer the questions.

In 1588, the Spanish Armada sailed to fight against England. The armada consisted of a fleet of 130 ships. Aboard one of these ships was a tailless cat. Her job was to catch mice. After a great naval battle that England dominated, the Spanish ships set sail for home. The cat's ship was wrecked near the Isle of Man. The nimble cat got ashore safely and lived there ever after. Her many descendants became known as Manx cats after the name of their island home. Manx cats are known for being tailless.

1 What was unusual about the cat in the Spanish Armada? _____

_____

2 What happened to the cat's ship? _____

_____

3 Where did the cat end up living? _____

_____

4 The title that best summarizes this paragraph is

Ⓐ Why Some Cats Are Tailless   Ⓒ How the Manx Cat Got Its Name

Ⓑ Why the Spanish Lost at Sea   Ⓓ Catching Mice Aboard a Ship

5 Use your answers to help you write a summary of the paragraph.

_____

_____

_____

Scholastic Teaching Resources   Main Ideas & Summarizing

Summarizing

Read the paragraph. Answer the questions.

Sailors have always needed lighthouses to warn them of dangerous conditions. The first tower that was built for such a purpose was at the entrance to Port Alexandria, a long-ago capital of ancient Egypt. The tower, called Pharos, was very large. It was so impressive a structure that it was known as one of the seven wonders of the ancient world. Fire beacons burning on the tower helped ships navigate through the treacherous waters approaching the city.

1 What was the name of the first lighthouse? _____

_____

2 Where was it located? _____

_____

3 Why was it a wonder? _____

_____

4 The title that best summarizes this paragraph is

Ⓐ Burning Fire Beacons in the Night   Ⓒ Helping Ships Navigate Tricky Waters

Ⓑ Pharos, the First Lighthouse Tower   Ⓓ A Look at Ancient Egypt

5 Use your answers to help you write a summary of the paragraph.

_____

_____

_____

Summarizing

Read the paragraph. Answer the questions.

Everyone knows that thousands of athletes compete in the Olympic Games and that
hundreds of thousands of visitors attend. But did you know that about 60,000 more
people work to make the Olympics run smoothly? Some of these workers are paid,
but thousands of others are volunteers. All of them have to be trained for their job.
These workers do everything from sweeping up litter to escorting competitors to
selling tickets to announcing winners.

1 Who make the Olympics run smoothly? _____

_____

2 How do these people know what to do? _____

_____

3 What kinds of jobs do these people do? _____

_____

4 The title that best summarizes this paragraph is

   Ⓐ How Athletes Compete at the Games   Ⓒ Tips for Visitors to the Olympics

   Ⓑ Working as a Ticket Seller   Ⓓ Workers Behind the Olympics

5 Use your answers to help you write a summary of the paragraph.

_____

_____

_____

Summarizing

Read the paragraph. Answer the questions.

What does it take to be a survivor? Gary Paulsen knows. This well-known writer had a difficult boyhood and left home at age 14. He worked with a carnival, on a farm, on a ranch, and as a truck driver. He's also been a teacher, editor, and singer. Today, Paulsen receives more than 400 letters a day from readers who identify with the struggles of the main character in his award-winning books, *Hatchet, Brian's Winter,* and *The River.* When he's not writing, Paulsen enjoys sailing and adventure.

1 Who is Gary Paulsen? _____

_____

2 What has his life been like? _____

_____

3 What is the main theme of his work? _____

_____

4 The title that best summarizes this paragraph is

   Ⓐ Reading Gary Paulsen's Books   Ⓒ Paulsen: Survivor in Life and Literature

   Ⓑ Why Paulsen Left Home at Age 14   Ⓓ Getting to Know Book Characters

5 Use your answers to help you write a summary of the paragraph.

_____

_____

_____

Summarizing

Read the paragraph. Answer the questions.

The explorer Marco Polo left his home in Italy in 1271. After many years of traveling, his party reached the summer palace of Kublai Khan in what is now China. Polo remained at the court for 17 years. He marveled at things not yet seen in Europe. For example, common people bathed daily. Roads and bridges were paved. People used paper money as currency. They also burned coal as a fuel. When Polo finally returned to Europe, it took a while before people believed the stories he told or the book he wrote about his travels.

1 Where did Marco Polo go? _____

_____

2 What amazed him? _____

_____

3 Why didn't people believe him on his return? _____

_____

4 The title that best summarizes this paragraph is

   Ⓐ What Marco Polo Was Like   Ⓒ A Wanderer From Italy

   Ⓑ Meeting Kublai Khan   Ⓓ The Travels of Marco Polo

5 Use your answers to help you write a summary of the paragraph.

_____

_____

_____

Summarizing

Read the paragraph. Answer the questions.

At one time, people thought that blowing dust was the way to clean. Then in the 1870s Hubert Booth, an engineer, tried placing a handkerchief between his mouth and a couch and sucking in. The film of dirt on the other side of the hanky suggested that suctioning in dirt was the way to clean. Booth designed fans that sucked dust into pillow cases. He even sold some to the Queen of England. About 30 years later, the Hoover Company came out with an upright suctioning machine on rollers. The rest is vacuum cleaner history.

1 Who was Hubert Booth? _____

_____

2 What did his experiment suggest? _____

_____

3 How did the Hoover Company improve on this concept? _____

_____

4 The title that best summarizes this paragraph is

(A) The First Vacuum Cleaners   (C) Blowing in the Dust

(B) How the Queen Cleaned   (D) What Hoover Did

5 Use your answers to help you write a summary of the paragraph.

_____

_____

_____

Summarizing

Read the paragraph. Answer the questions.

Some words are really combinations of two or more words. The new words are called blends. The meaning of a blend reflects the meanings of both words it comes from. For example, the words *gleam* and *shimmer* have been combined to make *glimmer*. The words *smoke* and *fog* blend to make *smog*. *Motor* and *cavalcade* combine to make *motorcade*. Can you figure out what *motor* and *hotel* make when combined? You're right—it's *motel*. What two words do you think *brunch* comes from?

1 What is a blend? _____

_____

2 How does a blend get its meaning? _____

_____

3 What are some examples of blends? _____

_____

4 The title that best summarizes this paragraph is

   Ⓐ Combining Smoke and Fog   Ⓒ How *Motel* Got Its Meaning

   Ⓑ Learning About Blends   Ⓓ Forming Compound Words

5 Use your answers to help you write a summary of the paragraph.

_____

_____

_____

Summarizing

Read the paragraph. Answer the questions.

You know that spiders spin silk, but do you know what spiders do with their silk? Mother spiders keep the eggs they lay in silk sacs. Spiders also use their silk to make webs or homes. Many spiders have hideouts in places such as window corners or under sills. They line the entrances to these places with silk. Spiders also use silk threads to drop straight to the ground when enemies appear. And, of course, spiders can spin silken traps and nets to catch their dinner.

1 How do spiders make homes? _____
_____

2 How do spiders stay safe? _____
_____

3 How do spiders catch food? _____
_____

4 The title that best summarizes this paragraph is

Ⓐ How Spiders Find Food   Ⓒ Spinning Silken Clothes

Ⓑ A Spider's Use of Silk   Ⓓ Outwitting Spider Enemies

5 Use your answers to help you write a summary of the paragraph.

_____
_____
_____

Summarizing

Read the paragraph. Answer the questions.

Music was very popular with the armies during the Civil War. Soldiers on both sides liked to gather around campfires and sing familiar songs such as "Home! Sweet Home!" and "'Tis the Last Rose of Summer." Confederate soldiers often sang "Dixie," while Northerners favored "Yankee Doodle." A song written especially for the war was "Battle Hymn of the Republic" by Julia Ward Howe. The bugle melody "Taps" was also first played as a sign-off to a soldier's day during the Civil War.

1 What songs were popular during the Civil War? _____

_____

2 What song was written for the war? _____

_____

3 What other song was introduced during the war? _____

_____

4 The title that best summarizes this paragraph is

(A) Singing "Home! Sweet Home!"   (C) Music of the Civil War

(B) The First Use of "Taps"   (D) Why Soldiers Like to Sing

5 Use your answers to help you write a summary of the paragraph.

_____

_____

_____

Scholastic Teaching Resources   Main Ideas & Summarizing

EXERCISE

28

Summarizing

Read the paragraph. Answer the questions.

In 1638, a Swedish ship arrived in America. The immigrants aboard founded a community called Fort Christina. The Dutch soon took over this settlement but not before the Swedes had built snug log cabins like those in their homeland. The cabins were made of notched logs carefully fitted together without nails. The walls were chinked with moss or clay, and the roofs were made of hardwood. Plentiful lumber made these easy-to-build cabins ideal for settlers. Log cabins became a symbol of the pioneer spirit.

1 Who brought the log cabin to America? _____

_____

2 How were the cabins made? _____

_____

3 Why were they ideal for settlers? _____

_____

4 The title that best summarizes this paragraph is

    Ⓐ A Building Boom in 1638   Ⓒ Contribution From the Dutch

    Ⓑ Building the Pioneer Spirit   Ⓓ Log Cabins From the Swedish

5 Use your answers to help you write a summary of the paragraph.

_____

_____

_____

Summarizing

Read the paragraph. Answer the questions.

Buddy was the first seeing-eye dog in the United States. Despite the name, she was really a female. This German shepherd was trained at a place called Fortunate Fields in Switzerland in the 1920s. Then she was matched with a blind American named Morris Frank. He and Buddy learned to work together. When they returned to the United States, Frank started a school to train more guide dogs. It was called the Seeing Eye. Today, the school is in Morristown, New Jersey. It matches 300 blind people with dogs like Buddy each year.

1 Who was Buddy? _____

_____

2 Who was Morris Frank? _____

_____

3 What did Frank start? _____

_____

4 The title that best summarizes this paragraph is

Ⓐ The First U.S. Seeing-Eye Dog   Ⓒ How Morris Frank Lost His Sight

Ⓑ A Furry Gift From Switzerland   Ⓓ Training at the Seeing Eye

5 Use your answers to help you write a summary of the paragraph.

_____

_____

_____

Scholastic Teaching Resources *Main Ideas & Summarizing*

Summarizing

Read the paragraph. Answer the questions.

Earthquakes cause buildings to fall and injure or kill people. So engineers and architects are trying to make buildings safer. Skyscrapers are built so that they sway but don't fall when earthquakes strike. Some buildings are put on rollers while others have steel beams anchored into the ground. Builders also use stronger and more flexible materials. A new idea is to put heavy weights in buildings so that if they move one way, the weight moves the other way to help keep the building from toppling.

1 How do earthquakes harm people? _____

_____

2 How do engineers try to make buildings safer? _____

_____

3 What new idea might help? _____

_____

4 The title that best summarizes this paragraph is

Ⓐ How Earthquakes Harm Us   Ⓒ Limiting Earthquake Damage

Ⓑ Why Skyscrapers Sway   Ⓓ Engineers and Architects at Work

5 Use your answers to help you write a summary of the paragraph.

_____

_____

_____

Summarizing

Read the paragraph. Answer the questions.

In the early years of the United States, land travel was difficult. Roads were no more than dirt paths that became rutted and muddy with rain. Finally, Congress decided to build a National Road. Work began at Cumberland, Maryland, in 1811. After seven years, the road stretched west to the Ohio River at Wheeling in what is now West Virginia. It wasn't until 1852 that the road reached its end at Vandalia, Illinois. In its time, thousands of settlers used the road to travel westward.

1 Why was a National Road built? _____

_____

2 Where and when did it begin and end? _____

_____

3 Who used the road? _____

_____

4 The title that best summarizes this paragraph is

    Ⓐ Traveling in America   Ⓒ Why Dirt Roads Don't Work

    Ⓑ Building the National Road   Ⓓ Who Used the National Road

5 Use your answers to help you write a summary of the paragraph.

_____

_____

_____

Scholastic Teaching Resources   *Main Ideas & Summarizing*

Summarizing

Read the paragraph. Answer the questions.

Turtles have been around for more than 200 million years. Scientists think they are the most ancient of all reptiles. Turtles live in many places on land and in water. Like all reptiles, they are cold-blooded. Turtles that live where winters are cold usually hibernate. Turtles eat insects, fish, and frogs. They also munch on plants, including fruit and flowers. The largest turtle is the leatherback, which can weigh more than 2,000 pounds!

1 How long have turtles existed? _____

_____

2 Where do turtles live? _____

_____

3 What do they eat? _____

_____

4 The title that best summarizes this paragraph is

Ⓐ Interesting Facts About Turtles   Ⓒ The Large Leatherback

Ⓑ Very Ancient Reptiles   Ⓓ Places Where Turtles Live

5 Use your answers to help you write a summary of the paragraph.

_____

_____

_____

Summarizing

Read the paragraph. Answer the questions.

Most communities have laws about how high fences can be in residential neighborhoods. Why? One reason is safety. Fences that are too high can block the view of motorists in driveways or near intersections. Another reason is that people tend to argue about fences that neighbors put up, saying they are unattractive or made of ugly materials. Fences can also restrict the rights of others by blocking views, light, or airflow. Good laws help settle such disputes.

1 How can fences be a safety problem? _____
_____

2 How can fences irritate neighbors? _____
_____

3 How can fences infringe on the rights of others? _____
_____

4 The title that best summarizes this paragraph is

Ⓐ Blocking Motorists' Views   Ⓒ Building Fences in Neighborhoods

Ⓑ Eliminating Ugly Fences   Ⓓ Why Communities Have Fence Laws

5 Use your answers to help you write a summary of the paragraph.

_____
_____
_____

Scholastic Teaching Resources   *Main Ideas & Summarizing*

Summarizing

Read the paragraph. Answer the questions.

The phrase *flotsam and jetsam* is often used to refer to the unfortunate in society. However, these words once referred to cargo found floating in water. Flotsam was cargo from a wrecked ship. Jetsam was cargo that was purposely thrown overboard either to lighten the ship's load or to keep the goods from going down with the ship. Jetsam belonged to the ship's owner. Anything that was flotsam belonged to the government.

1 What does *flotsam and jetsam* mean today? _____

_____

2 What was flotsam? _____

_____

3 What was jetsam? _____

_____

4 The title that best summarizes this paragraph is

Ⓐ Society's Less Fortunate   Ⓒ Learning About Flotsam

Ⓑ Story of Flotsam and Jetsam   Ⓓ Cargo From Shipwrecks

5 Use your answers to help you write a summary of the paragraph.

_____

_____

_____

EXERCISE
35

Summarizing

Read the paragraph. Answer the questions.

When a hockey player scores three goals in a row with no other goals scored by other players, it is called a "hat trick." Where did this expression come from? It was originally used in the English game of cricket to describe a bowler taking three wickets on successive balls. The reward for such a feat was often a new hat. Sometimes fans passed a hat and took up a collection for the player who scored so well. The term "hat trick" soon spread to other sports, including soccer and hockey.

1 What is a "hat trick" in hockey? _____

_____

2 From what sport did the term come? _____

_____

3 What do hats have to do with the term? _____

_____

4 The title that best summarizes this paragraph is

   Ⓐ How to Score a Hockey Game   Ⓒ The History of "Hat Trick"

   Ⓑ How Players Win Hats   Ⓓ Sports With "Hat Tricks"

5 Use your answers to help you write a summary of the paragraph.

_____

_____

_____

Scholastic Teaching Resources · Main Ideas & Summarizing

Main Ideas

Read the paragraphs. Circle the sentence that tells the main idea. Then write a title that tells about the main idea.

1 _____

(title)

Horses do almost all of their sleeping while standing up. Some horses stand for a month at a time! When standing, a horse's legs lock to provide a kind of sling for the weight of its body. The leg muscles are relaxed, and the horse doesn't have to exert energy to remain standing. Experts think that standing while sleeping began with wild horses as a means of defense. Speed was a horse's greatest asset in escaping an enemy. A horse was less likely to be caught by surprise when standing; it was ready to run.

2 _____

(title)

A surname is a family or last name. The U.S. Census Bureau reports that Smith is the most common surname in the country. Although Hispanic names such as Garcia and Martinez are becoming more and more common, Smith has been at the top of the list for about 50 years. Originally, the name was given to someone who worked with metal, and many countries had such people. Schmidt, Schmitt, Smed, and Szmyt are just a few versions of Smith in other languages.

Summarizing

Read the paragraphs. Circle the sentence that tells the main idea. Then write a few sentences to summarize the paragraphs.

Consumers often spend a few puzzled moments looking at egg cartons in supermarkets. That's because there are six official egg sizes. The sizes are determined by weight. A jumbo, the largest-size egg, weighs 30 ounces while a peewee egg, the smallest size, weighs only 15 ounces. In between are extra-large, large, medium, and small eggs. Most markets only stock the four largest sizes; small and peewee eggs are usually sold to bakers and companies in the food processing business.

1 _____

_____

_____

People take cars and other road vehicles for granted today. However, the idea of such vehicles was unheard of about 500 years ago. Then, in 1478, the artist and inventor Leonardo da Vinci designed a self-propelled vehicle. His drawing showed a boxy, open-topped wooden machine with three wheels. Coiled springs would make the vehicle move somewhat like a windup toy. Models of Leonardo's vehicle have been made in recent years and are on exhibit in museums in Italy.

2 _____

_____

_____

Name _____   Date _____

Student Record

Date	Exercise #	Number Correct	Comments

Answers

page 8:
1. how snakes move
2. Answers will vary.
3. Answers will vary.
4. Answers will vary.

page 9:
1. grand canyons in the United States
2. Answers will vary.
3. Answers will vary.
4. Answers will vary.

page 10:
1. C
2. B
3. A
4. B

page 11:
1. D
2. C
3. B
4. B

page 12:
1. B
2. D
3. C
4. D

page 13:
1. C
2. A
3. D
4. D

page 14:
1. A
2. D
3. C
4. B

page 15:
1. D
2. B
3. B
4. A

page 16:
1. C
2. C
3. A
4. D

page 17:
1. B
2. A
3. D
4. C

page 18:
1. B
2. C
3. D
4. A

page 19:
1. D
2. B
3. A
4. B

page 20:
1. A
2. C
3. A
4. C

page 21:
1. B
2. D
3. D
4. C

page 22:
1. C
2. A
3. C
4. B

page 23:
1. C
2. B
3. D
4. A

page 24:
1. D
2. A
3. B
4. C

page 25:
1. B
2. C
3. A
4. D

page 26:
1. A
2. D
3. C
4. A

page 27:
1. A
2. B
3. C
4. D

page 28:
1. It was tailless.
2. It was shipwrecked.
3. on the Isle of Man
4. C
5. Summaries should include information from answers 1–4.

page 29:
1. Pharos
2. at the entrance to Port Alexandria
3. It was large and impressive.
4. B
5. Summaries should include information from answers 1–4.

page 30:
1. 60,000 workers
2. They are trained.
3. sweep litter, escort competitors, sell tickets, announce winners

4. D
5. Summaries should include information from answers 1–4.

page 31:
1. He's an author.
2. He had a hard boyhood and has worked at many different jobs.
3. survival
4. C
5. Summaries should include information from answers 1–4.

page 32:
1. China
2. People bathed daily, roads were paved, people used paper money, people burned coal as fuel.
3. They hadn't seen or heard of such things.
4. D
5. Summaries should include information from answers 1–4.

page 33:
1. He was an engineer.
2. It suggested that suctioning in dirt was a better way to clean than blowing it.
3. It made an upright vacuum on rollers.
4. A
5. Summaries should include information from answers 1–4.

page 34:
1. It is a combination of two or more words.
2. It reflects meaning from both words it comes from.
3. motel, smog, brunch, glimmer, motorcade
4. B
5. Summaries should include information from answers 1–4.

page 35:
1. They spin webs.
2. They have hideouts and they use silk threads to drop to the ground when enemies appear.
3. They spin silk traps.
4. B
5. Summaries should include information from answers 1–4.

page 36:
1. "Home! Sweet Home!," "'Tis the Last Rose of Summer," "Dixie," "Yankee Doodle"

2. "Battle Hymn of the Republic"
3. "Taps"
4. C
5. Summaries should include information from answers 1–4.

page 37:
1. The Swedes
2. They were made of notched logs fitted together without nails and chinked with clay or moss.
3. Wood was plentiful and they were easy to build.
4. D
5. Summaries should include information from answers 1–4.

page 38:
1. She was the first guide dog in the United States.
2. He was her master.
3. A school called the Seeing Eye
4. A
5. Summaries should include information from answers 1–4.

page 39:
1. They cause buildings to fall and hurt people.
2. Skyscrapers sway, some buildings are on rollers, others are anchored. Builders use stronger, more flexible materials.
3. Weights
4. C
5. Summaries should include information from answers 1–4.

page 40:
1. Dirt roads were difficult to travel on.
2. It began in Cumberland, Maryland, in 1811 and ended in 1852 in Vandalia, Illinois.
3. settlers
4. B
5. Summaries should include information from answers 1–4.

page 41:
1. 200 million years
2. on land and in water
3. insects, fish, frogs, plants
4. A
5. Summaries should include information from answers 1–4.

page 42:
1. They can block the view of motorists at driveways and intersections.
2. People may think they are unattractive.
3. By restricting views, light, airflow
4. D
5. Summaries should include information from answers 1–4.

page 43:
1. the unfortunate in society
2. It was cargo that floated after a shipwreck.
3. It was cargo thrown overboard.
4. B
5. Summaries should include information from answers 1–4.

page 44:
1. It is three goals in a row by one player with no other goals scored in between.
2. cricket
3. Hats were rewarded to bowlers who took three wickets on successive balls; sometimes hats were passed around for a collection.
4. C
5. Summaries should include information from answers 1–4.

page 45:
1. Possible title: Why Horses Sleep Standing Up. Main idea sentence: Horses do almost all of their sleeping while standing up.
2. Possible title: The Name Smith Tops the List; Main idea sentence: The U.S. Census Bureau reports that Smith is the most common surname in the country.

page 46:
1. Main idea sentence: There are six official egg sizes. Summaries will vary.
2. Main idea sentence: Then, in 1478, the artist and inventor Leonardo da Vinci designed a self-propelled vehicle. Summaries will vary.